EMMA NEALE

has published five novels and three
collections of poetry. She has edited three anthologies:
Creative Juices (HarperCollins, 2001), *Best New Zealand Poems* 2004
and *Swings and Roundabouts: Poems on Parenthood* (Godwit, 2007). Her
poetry has appeared in UK, Australian and New Zealand periodicals, and
extracts of her work have appeared in North American literary publications
such as *Bat City Review*, the *Harvard Review*, and the website *Poetry Daily*.
A past recipient of the Creative New Zealand/Todd New Writers' Bursary,
she was awarded the inaugural NZSA/Janet Frame Memorial Award for
Literature, and is the 2012 Robert Burns Fellow at the University of
Otago. Her most recent novel, *Fosterling*, is shortlisted for the
Sir Julius Vogel Award for Science Fiction
and Fantasy.

THE
KATHLEEN GRATTAN
AWARD FOR POETRY
2011

The Truth Garden

Poems by Emma Neale

OTAGO

With thanks to the Kathleen Grattan Estate and Trustees

The Truth Garden is the fourth book in the series arising from the Kathleen Grattan Award for Poetry. The award was established with a bequest by Jocelyn Grattan, in memory of her mother, who was a poet, journalist and editor. Each book is produced with attention to the traditional qualities of fine book production, in typography, illustration, design, paper and binding. This book was illustrated by Kathryn Madill, designed by Fiona Moffat, and is set in
Footlight 10/13.5.

Published by Otago University Press
PO Box 56/Level 1, 398 Cumberland Street
Dunedin, New Zealand
Fax: 64 3 479 8385. Email: university.press@otago.ac.nz
First published 2012
Copyright © Emma Neale 2012
ISBN 978 1 877578 25 0
Printed in Hong Kong through Condor Production Ltd

POEMS

Good Morning, Miss   9

Jumpy   10

Discontinuous   12

New Year, New You   13

Satellite   15

Farewell Do   16

The Last Yoga Class   17

Haunted   19

'This too will pass'   20

Wrought   21

Fall   22

Don't Stay Up Too Late, Love   23

Fidelity Sestina   25

Loops   27

An Inward Sun 28

Event! 29

No Time Like the Present 31

Portrait of the Artist as a Young Wolf 32

Girls' High 33

On the death of a daughter 34

Engulfed 35

Toothed Moon 36

Dormant 37

Open Air Theatre 39

So Long 40

Hound 41

Growth 42

Brood 43

Snails 45

Well 48

Rootstock 49

Proposal 51

Charm 52

Little Drummer Boy 54

Mind's Eye 56

Seismograph 57

Mourning Song 59

Late 60

Heron Blue 61

Instructions for a Karitane Solo: How to Use this Crib 63

Acknowledgements 64

Good Morning, Miss

As she speaks, the sky goes drowsy as rata laden with bees
and some fine dust seems to trickle over your limbs
so your skin nearly hums with hunger for sleep.

She's been there, too, where you sit,
chin propped on one hand, knees crossed,
so one foot swings as you kick and rock
like a dinghy loosely tethered by its prow,
heart pulling at your chest, wild pony in a harness,
wanting this hour of 'whys' and 'hows' to end,
so the time of your life can begin,
when every molecule of self will fizz and ring with *now*.

Even though she can see you dream of a dozen other things:
carnivals, parades; a sprint down the street;
an open-field dance, the green leap of waves;
the place you might meet the one whose name
you would doodle all day in blue and blue and blue,

she keeps up her talk
as if to coax some small animal from its crawlspace,
or a lonely man back from some high ledge,
for she trusts (she has been there) that one day

when you stop in your hot kitchen
as the children mill like kittens at your feet,
or you step alone down a dirt road at night,
where moths flicker above the darkened grass—
gold dots and dashes in the torch's Morse—
or you wait in a foreign city on a crowded train,
and you are lost in some intimate, troubled thought,

her words, which have travelled all this time,
patient as photons from some remote star,
will spill like incandescence around your hands
and you will hear her, you will hear her,
see clearly where you need to be, and are.

Jumpy

Upstairs a baby sleeps
we turn to other work

but find we have grown fish skin:
nerves flicker with every vibration

mistake the neighbour's power tool
for the waking cry

mistake a car's uphill grind
for the waking cry

mistake a bellbird's carillon
for the waking cry

mistake a distant factory's whistle
for the waking cry

mistake the cat's whine and yawl
for the waking cry

mistake a branch rocking in the wind
for the waking cry

mistake the drone of a trapped bee
for the waking cry:

and here, in our hands
as we pass it between us,
it seems newborn:
covered in soft lanugo fuzz,
legs in bumbly doggy-paddle
it tries to keep its head up

in deep blue air
too small, surely, to be left out alone
under the vast and open sky
can't you almost catch its voice,
thrown out in a high thin arc
like a silver rope flung
from a drenched and listing ship

ah no
it is the waking cry
we release the bee
its legs scramble
on the sill of the window;
we all run
for sweet life.

Discontinuous

I have a friend who has a wish
for life to be discontinuous:
to save up some of these hours,
spend them later, in the heart's rain,
decades from now;

or, next month, how about life takes a loan,
subtracts a hoard of days from old age?
Tuesday and Wednesday might suit:
days for her to sit, think, rock and stitch,
listen to the wind, the steel-brush of sleet,
the trickle of hail melt from the eaves,
as her mind carefully traces and retraces these days
to get them by heart,
the exact turn of phrase
that could hurtle her back even farther
to nineteen, twenty, its vigorous dance,
the inevitable
where-did-it-go toboggan to this
talk over coffee and cake
as our sons, gentle giants in miniature,
play *you be the builder, I'll be the driver,
then you be the boy, I'll be the father ...
quick as catch can, boys, before the years come.*

New Year, New You

For Zachariah Dylan Baillie

Your age still just counted in days,
you're the newest you you'll ever be:

face smooth as an unstamped moon cake,
self already coiled
far down inside your sleep
like a tight spool of rice paper
printed with a ladder of ideograms
it will take us years of study to understand:

the marks for the patient ox's
hard-labouring heart, perhaps,
or for some sweetly-foxing paradox,
like a man's large appetite for solitude
alongside his fiery, tigerish devotions …

or maybe, written along the blue, flexible web
spun under your skin
are signs we'll decipher sooner:

the code for a child running through nose-tickling grass,
its seed heads darting like a hundred rabbits' scuts;
for a boy who scales trees bent over earth
like a mother's and father's spines;
for the shared tenderness of a brother
whose limbs knew *dance* before they knew *walk*;
or for your seven-year-old self
rescuing cicadas from the jaws of the cat,
wearing them pinned to the skin of your wrists
like bright green watches, a bandit's loot,
or a double-agent's evil spy devices …

Watching the soft candle-pulse
behind your skull's thin screen
already we make our wish:
that you'll know shelter, long life, love's green seasons—
for here, give us the fists you keep pursed as tight
as white, five-cloved bulbs:
feel how something loosens and lifts
like lanterns glued from red paper packets
sent to float out over the city's dark hills
which tonight are curved like a newborn's head
pressed close to a nightgown cut from space,
and stained wet with a spill of stars.

Satellite

Our six-year-old watches me dress
as we talk about the planets,
where rockets have landed,
where people can't go,
how the surface of some distant Earth
is unknowable at the moment

and he frowns and stares
with a mathematician's intent
from breast to breast
as they tip into their bra cups
and I slip the hooks shut,
flip the straps straight;

he reads me fast and furious
there is something urgent
he must remember here
some fresh store of data he must make
if he's to save the World, the Good Force, himself,
before the lid of time's capsule slides shut
and he's shot right out of boyhood's orbit
the mother-ship shucked like a shell that's shrunk
with no sound but his own breath in his ears.

Farewell Do

There are the sweet cakes, the streamers,
the flush-cheeked children who think today
is about the sweet cakes, the streamers.

There is the beautifully aloof, heartless sunshine;
likewise the bare-armed hills, crowned in azaleas
like extrovert brides; the city's thin, quiet streets
their safe-choice grooms

and all of us standing around, throats
stoppered with a hot knot,
a hard thought that's locked there

hands loose and empty, no casket to carry,
of course it's not as bad as all that,
yet when we wave and call 'goodbye, good luck,'

the car doors' *thud, thud-thud,*
their soft sombre tom-tom,
fills our backs and arms with a slow ache:
ghost of love's last, awful weight.

The Last Yoga Class

We're all lying on the floor
on carpet that smells of wool
and shoes and dust and rain.
It's at the end, the part where we're
supposed to empty our heads
of all those negative thoughts—
the negative thoughts, it always seems,
that love an empty head—

when the teacher says, *clear your mind,*
if a problem arises, don't get sticky with it.
Let it all go.

So I try.
In my corner of the room
to the sound of my neighbours' breaths
like tired ships barely cresting waves
I look up through the window
at clouds in their slow dance of veils

and think
how frightening it would be
if that big blue screen just
powered down and flickered out
to leave us all here
blind as worms in an alien soil ...

but the instructor's voice says
none of it matters
don't get sticky with it, just let it all go

so I do, I let it go and
all the other thoughts and worries push in
they soar and race like shape-changing cumulus
but to each one I try to say
goodbye
goodbye worries about our children's future

goodbye work concerns

goodbye creative struggle

goodbye poor sick planet, and the rainbow
of species that never asked for this

goodbye to the hours from now to ever after

goodbye love, goodbye

goodbye sweet everything

which I think is probably when
I first feel able to let
yoga class go.

Haunted

Sudden
sadness finds you, fills your skullbone's cup;
dumping love it runs like water
falling hillside gutters, rushes, tumbles,
carries facts and time's sweet healing
past either ken or sense … *I'm life*
swears insistent melancholy, *I'm truth.*

Viral fever craving hosts,
sadness slinks and spawns,
insinuates between each breath.
Self is landscape, sadness says:
some draw darkness sure as valleys.

Reason? There's no good one.
Anywhere, any time,
sadness calls you like some wrong-crowd friend:
secret pact you're blooded to.
So here, on the streets of Anytown,
you're drenched
in your own ghost's cold skin.

'This too will pass'

Snowflake locks on to snowflake,
hook into eyelet.

Beneath the killing coat
pressed over the garden
like fever over a baby's mouth:

the polite yellow cup and saucer sets
of daffodils,
the fat red clutch of tulips.

How ludicrous.

As improbable that love could grow
through sickness and fear;
that love could last
past sickness and fear.

Yet the seasons speak.
Our selves melt, run, dissipate.

You are not who you were.
From year to year:
incredible resurrection.

See the grown child come running
with chips of frost on his woollen mittens,
hands held open
like astonishment;

overnight, beauty descends
on its invisible trajectory,
to leave such as these seed pearls
that ache and shimmer
with the cool grain of identity.

Wrought

It is as if you are the film
that night draws over each day,

the skin the mind must peel
from every thought.

Even in sleep your name rises, taut, milkwhite,
and pulls me from sweet numbness

like a cool, insistent moon
with its steady inquisition.

Its syllables of light
have the unwanted hooks

of songs I'd best forget.
Your eyes, your mouth, your voice:

these, love, are what the ancient laws
were wrought against,

on stones to make a stopbank
against the heart's anarchic tides.

Fall

When it happened
was it just that I was standing
in the place where your light fell?

Your random, animal love
for the world:
mountain, harbour,
birch trees, song-lilt, star-shot,
sea-sway, eyelash, gumnut,
sunbeams aflash off roofs on the far hills
or caught and lobbed as a window opens

as if my body, mind, speech, too were spun glass:
a vessel, each, for something found equally
in the lakes, streams, passing crowd,
music score, spinning, scarlet leaf …

Day fades. Love fades. The mirror drains,
no longer throws its fiery signals,
light talking to light,
leaping, like a heart.

Don't Stay Up Too Late, Love

Night, and the study window burns
not like a beacon, but as if to warn
late travellers from some hidden reef

of thought: how to stockpile time, how hoard its shine
when time's the very stuff that seeps inside us,
red web that spiders from the heart.

Cars pass the house: none stops, as if piloted by
mariners who already know melancholia's bleak shoals.
Yet something does slow:

half a dozen moths, the window's chill glass
their rink, their stage.
They see this man is an island of light.

They skate across the white-lit screen:
a ballet corps in copper and gold
they toe-dance, tap-dance, *pas de papillon de nuit,*

pirouette and quiet morse, grand jêté and semaphore,
wild as seabirds but precise as needlepoint
they spit like sparks from a campfire's heart.

Their wing-flickers signal
how hard it is to reach across
the cold skin between the mind and its ideal;

they shadow-act the wife who stands
behind him in the doorway
as she waits, watches, tries to speak
across the distance between long love, its first dream.

And yet, as they lance the midnight air
like flakes of sun that fall through trees
they seem to ask what brighter beauty is there

than in this striving, the effort of the dance?

Fidelity Sestina

In one of those typical young couples' games
when we first made house we used to wonder aloud
what we'd do if one of us fell off love
and under with someone else, the very word *affair*
almost scalding our mouths, like a backstage
hex, love's *Macbeth*. After all our imaginings ('I'd want to try again,'

'I'd leave,' 'I'd cry,' 'I'd be sick') we'd have to exorcise the curse again:
kiss, cling, swear the game's
not over yet, and why should it ever be a stage
we'd have to go through, when each of us allowed
the other to seek what seemed most fine and fair
to follow: the bliss outside us both that helps give love

room as we bring home happiness that's also thanks for love.
It's the old adage all over again:
hen or egg, shell or feathers? Love enables, but perhaps it's fair
to say that freer lovers are abler, too. Strange how those painful mind games
we'd been locked in before—you with a hot-headed, a loud
angry woman, me with a tall Peter Pan who loved the stage

(people said adolescence was the lifelong stage
he'd be stalled in)—we took to be a natural part of love,
the cost of being allowed
to share another person's life again,
now we thought we'd grown out of the old coat of our own families, their
                                                        games-
cupboards, junk sheds, go-carts, chores, the unspoken sores it's a fair

bet every family has and thinks their own affair.
Now those days seem melodramatic, stagey,
the young heart acting out its own elaborate game,
a practice, dress-up version of adult love.
Only, whenever we'd fought with those ex-es again
about what was and wasn't allowed

with other men, other women—'allowed'
said as if lovers were parent substitutes, 'affair'
as if it were every injustice we'd ever felt, now met again
in the shape of lover as a morality-play's stage
villain—it sometimes seemed that love
was the worst thing to be in: a blood-sport hunt, with us the game.

I never thought love would mean I could say, if you were ever to have an
                                                                                    affair,
I hope I'd see sometimes life just has to stage a love of itself again.
Pray I'm game enough to concede, the heart's allowed so few dances, let it
                                                                                    play,
let it play, till its brief light's done.

Loops

When I tell my child
of the dream I had
where he was lost—

he'd gone alone
down to the water;
and I loosely, numbly, let too long lapse
before cold alarm set in
and made me run
down to the deep, green pools,
the rocks and weed so stark and still
as if to say how clear the horror
of his calm, floating face would be—

he told me it wasn't real,
it can't have been,
because while I dreamed
he was somewhere else;

that is, in a different dream:
of another boy's house,
dancing in costumes of moths and magicians,
eating cakes shaped like small circus marquees,
so I mustn't be sad: he was happy, and safe,
at a party a long, long way from the sea.

An Inward Sun

A small, pale circle
shimmers on the kitchen bench
darts to the wall,
drops back to the floor
where it pulses
quick with fear and warm life.

The cat tries to pat it and pluck it:
sniffs, perhaps thinks
of the furred, golden heart
of a field mouse; butter-fried yolk;
round of Gouda; scrap of Sunday pancake.

The baby wants to work the trick
it thinks the cat in its catness can't:
tries to pinch the sun spill up
between finger and thumb;
licks at the honey trickle look
as it pools on the back of his hand,
and so grows the belief
that if he could touch his tongue to the sun
it would taste of popsicle melt,
beach grit, hind-milk, skin-salt
and a whiskery, shadowy,
trace element of cat.

Event!

A road sign by the footpath warns Event!
I think—oh—accident, disruption,
the day wrenched from its socket;
brace for some sudden lurch or dash,
the heart's mayhem or high distress;
slow and scan the road

but all there is to see
is a man hunting through his bag
on the overbridge—
for a bomb? Will he jump?
No, he shoulders his pack
and walks on, whistling
under the warm copper wheel of the sun.

There's some other traffic
in a slow motion mosey
but otherwise, just me:
this cyclist biking past
thinking Event!

And now I see it:
the harbour glistens,
a shoal of ripples flares
along its massive green hide
like scattered silver shavings;

the bicycle pumps and glides
as if it's never felt more alive;
wind sings through its spokes
in the dearly off-key hum
of love pottering in a sun-spilled room.

Event!
It's this nothing particular moment
strung from here to there
inexplicable happiness
dissolved along the blood
as if some old god
has descended in a shower of gold,
turned the body into a bead of light
run on a wire of air.

No Time Like the Present

No present like time
to follow thought's curving rivers,
divert down their sidecreeks and braidways,
catch the glint of a song, an answer
turning in their currents;
to revolve, resolve,
and there make the best of ourselves …

So if I could, I would give you time:
first a clutch of hours,
next a sprig of days,
then, for some significant occasion
a whole crate of months
left on your doorstep
without a note, or a name—

and though you might go to your gate,
scan the street, it would yield no sign:
puzzled, you'd sigh, turn back,
open the crate—

only to find yourself
      months later

whistling happily, smiling at the air
for no apparent reason, other than
here's another capacious day
its blue-kisses-blue horizon
tugging at your mind

the way the wind begs a skiff
out onto a dance floor
the sun has waxed
bright as water.

Portrait of the Artist as a Young Wolf

After reading 'On Film' by Martin Edmond

He says one of his 'more louche ambitions'
was to wear his gumboots to a small-town matinée.

Louche: from sideways, not straightforward
but it whispers with loose, *loup, bouche,*
the mouth's ripe, careless outline, sleek and savage.

Watch him, tousled, unshaven, as he pads and paces,
hunkers on his haunches in the cinema's dark den
in the smells of salt and fear, hope and sex;
he nuzzles at the air as the backrow heads press together

and before he springs
(to leave behind those ridiculous, outsized shoes)
see his eyes: two yellow, angled mirrors
for his pretty, hourglass targets;
see his teeth glint in the projector's stuttering beam
as he leaps to rip off the half-masks of loveliness.

And still, down the years, stalks the truth
with an elegance wild, uncompromising
wolverine.

Girls' High

Gridlines and hairclips, bus rides and wooden desks, uniforms and regular verbs, shoe polish and irrational numbers, shoulder bags and fire drills, ponytails and violins, peroxide and clarinet, headaches and flashing lights, itchy skin, ink blots, sore spots, Cornish pasties and custard squares for the School Dux's lunch, cup of 1 cal soup and lo-salt cracker for the Most Successful Anorexic, volleyballs and potters' wheels, Bunsen burners and glass beakers, poster-paint and stage-boards, stomach cramps and gym skirts, *True Confessions* magazines with pretty cover nuns, Attic vases and roller skates, chalk dust and white boards, insomnia and Clearasil, homework and concrete steps, forbidden lifts and shirts pulled out, knuckle down and buck up, best friends and breakups, last bus and movie dates, French kiss and roll your Rs, boyfriends and sleepyheads, buck down and knuckle up, Glandular Fever and bomb scares, delicious rumours and bitten-back tears, silver cups and eyeliners, favourite bands and cosine, socials, cordial and rum 'n' coke, changing-room sweat, swimming caps and church bells, skirts wind-lifted, exam nerves and tampons, chewing gum and chamber music, assemblies and honour board, cut lawns and mufti days, pot smoke behind locked loo doors, permanent expulsions and liquid suspensions, crosscurrents and roll your eyes, leotards and leg warmers, fainting spells and spelling *feint*, permission slip and orthodontics, tarty arse and prune face, quadratic equations and Martian invasions, moon-raking and mocking-stock cannon fodder, starter guns and piano chords, parabolas and hyperbole, doodle hearts, achey braces, broken zips and allergies, swelling hips on the march for nuclear free, heart shaky in your knees, sink or swim at lunch time, home room and tuck shop, scared limp and bold as class, model student drop out got a job as a model for a postal shopping catalogue, box pleats flibbertigibbet, ice-numb earlobes pin-pierced hepatitis site, parent-teacher interviews, parent preach-you interludes, orange peel, white out, percentages, vocab lists, teachers' Mona Lisa smiles hide a thousand desires, the days built up like sandcastles, swept over by the moon white as foam, still you feel them wash up again from the dim-darks to the where-you-are, in this hot rewinding coil.

On the death of a daughter

Nowadays often he finds himself down at the river
with fishing rods and home-made lures
that dance as colour-drenched and flamboyant
as an opera diva's earrings
though the gear, and the catch (if any) aren't the point.

He goes because he has to.
Because sometimes a twig floats by,
or a bird jags past,
or a dragonfly balances
on thin air.

And it's—

    he cannot finish what it is.

Yet in this still room
we feel the river move on and on
as if there were comfort
in something pushing forward from its source,
always forward,
light gleaming on its surface instant after instant,
each sudden vision—leaf, water-beetle, seed-pod—
a match that is struck against a deep-running dark.

Engulfed

Cycling after sundown,
fear and doubt crystallising on the horizon
like the scent of winter,
he tackles a hill, reaches the summit,
catches full sweep of the port city's lights:

a myriad minds burn away
at their own urgent errands of living
Rome fiddles and burns, fiddles and burns.

As he swoops home
the darkness detaches a leaf of itself:
some small nocturnal creature draws ahead
then slips back under the night's cold surface

and with dream-logic
there's some deeper release
a poor and hampering, sorrowful piece set free
as if all the heart's pathlessness,
the hurt world's wider harms,
could be eased
as readily as breath mists on stillness
and some time soon
every patch of sadness, fret and harried
will just drift away,
their strange, long work done

for the world will no more need us
homo nocens,

than the animal who spoons itself
from shadow to shadow
as stealthily, we imagine,
as a single life vanishes:
intangible honey
trickled
from the body's deep comb.

Toothed Moon

'Even now this landscape is assembling ... as the toothed moon rises'
'All Hallows', Louise Glück

Last night your father took you out into the dark in his arms, and held you beneath the tall blue eucalyptus that stood like pillars cut from shadow. For the first time in your short life, he showed you the true moon and stars, whose names you can say more clearly than your own, and whose copies you have seen and sung from a dozen books and rhymes. Star, in fact, was your first word, though 'moon' had to grow slowly from 'spoon'. This made me imagine you had already seen the moon itself like a great ladle that cradled warm, breast-white light in the sky. But just as you craned your head right back, to drink in the immensity of space, the neighbours' dogs began to bay. Panic jammed you in its clamp. Sound, sudden as a gun, seemed to blast a hole right through the night: a hole that could pull you in, swiftly as the sky swallows up balloons. You clung tighter and tighter to your father, and shivered, though the day's heat still lingered in the air like a scent on the night's skin. When he brought you inside, and I tried to soothe you, too, you seemed only to take fiercer hold: monkey to its mother as she flees from tree to tree while the jungle burns. And though I finally calmed you, and helped you slide off to sleep, twice you woke, far into the night, with the chill scream of a small furred thing caught in a claw hooked like a sickle, stared down by a white, loveless eye. So I hunkered low in the shape of comfort, and I held you, and I hushed you, as if I wasn't afraid. As if I wasn't afraid.

Dormant

We've let the children overhear us fret
about the state of the world to come
but it's been a beautiful day,
they're not scared, they've already decided
the best thing for it is to get on ahead
with growing up, by which time
together they'll have perfected
one single magnificent glinting invention
to defend the entire planet.

These two small braves want each other to stay the night:
there's no time to waste,
they'll get back to work the minute they wake—
of course we do what adults must do,
and drive all the normal, boring, reassuring bargains:
if you bathe, if you're in bed by eight, then yes,
you can be our only hope, you can save the world.

Freshly showered, towelled, brushed and buttoned
they shuffle down into sleeping-bag talk:
secrets brothers, scheme brothers,
plot brothers, what-if brothers,
they lay their imaginations down side by side,
thin blades in the blood-black night,
press their words to each other
warm as wrists;
and as they slow into sleep,
they look at me with such wild happy tired faces
it's true they seem like kin.

Yet later, as I slipper in to place extra blankets over them,
our visitor looks unlike even himself.
Pale and luminous as moon paring,
he's still, stiller than ever I've seen him:
the daylight-child is all monkey firecracker popcorn slingshot
cap-gun balloon bang star-jump star-jump,
fence-straddle wrestle-tackle rabbit-shot shortcut

how d'y'spell parallel I'm hungry eat that
more please Lego base chocolate face snowball fight
dogstick dogfetch what's that I found
penknife whittle-trap supple-jack possum-track—

his silence now a soft shock:
he's fallen back into himself
like a fountain turned down

and as if dreams can lift from the clean scalps of boys
the way fragrance steals from night jasmine
I find I wish and I wish
I could snip a wisp of his fox-gold hair,
add an ash-blond curl of my son's,
press them into the hurt earth like balm,
and, as in some new myth, have the locks spring up
in an army of calm:
lenient as trees bent in thought,
hearts branched against the dark.

Open Air Theatre

A wild day for a walk by the shore, the blue wind scours the sky
like a metal so bright it makes us wince,
and we wonder why we've shouldered this weather,
what makes us think we need such punishment,
when a black shape spits sky-wise from the harbour's tongue
then drifts back down towards the water
like a burnt emergency flare.

Startled to a stop, we think we're seeing something,
and we are, it's really something:
the wind rears up, hurls the spent flotsam
high as the mollymawks and gulls,
where its four dark fronds un-origami into a man.

Lung-whoop, throat-yodel, wetsuit-slick and kite-board flipping,
he's popcorn shot from hot pan fat,
a circus geezer strapped to his trapeze,
Olympic gymnast in a spritzy floor-dance,
backwards parachutist who crows *Ominorej!* on the updraught,
thistle-up and whistle-down we can clock the wind by.

He lifts and limps, soars and flails, acts a life's melodrama
in clownish fast-forward:
he wants to be the squall's punch-drunk puppet,
transcribe the giddy arc of a mayfly-elation.
His kite's a balloon that swoons over and over
lust-drunk, then bitch-dumped, like a bad-love addict—

but, ally-oop, ally-up, up and at 'em:
the way his sway-ful bravery plays it,
even the collapse is so balletic, operatic,
we can almost believe it's each failure
that fills his rise with *can't breathe* beauty.

So Long

My friend has a friend, one of those 'just-friends' friends,
and every time I see him, he needs to tell me how it goes:
no urge to do so for any other friend
and the neat, uncomplicated nothing-between-them.

He asks, if they said everything they haven't said,
would there be any need to meet again?
Each time they do, there's a table, a newspaper,
and everything not said between them.

Gently as a seedling thumbs its green key
through the earth's soft lock
into the jazz rush of air and sun,
the silence opens with everything not said between them.

Where once there was only easy talk, the chatter of facts,
now their eyes meet, seem to fit sweet as hip to hip,
and by the light of their own gaze, for a moment,
see everything not said between them.

They've never touched and never will,
because *responsible* and *strive to be true*
are just some of the values that stand aside
from everything not said between them.

Yet, he says, he wonders if what he'll have to resist,
when he looks back
at how the friendship has shaped and changed him,
is that what he'll want to quote her on

won't be the store of conversations traded,
nor that they were friends so long,
but the slow, sensual lure, the plunge and lift
of everything never said between them.

Hound

The heart's a bitch.
It's caught the scent of your coat hem,
the tang of leather and metal on your wrists,
the soft skin at your neck
where the blood's cursor flashes.

You've gone
leaving no clear sign—
but still the heart strains and whines
wants off the leash,
snout like a cool, black magnet
clinched to the invisible print
of where you passed

as if it would track you
bring you to the ground
stunned but unbloodied
the light on your face
the sheen of wet freesias
as the warm jaws lie you
like long, green stems
at my feet.

Growth

Nodules, tumours, chemo, oncologist:
a harsh jargon it's hard to think your way clear through
when pain closes in with its harsh white haze.

We read your careful message
and find all we're left with
is a primitive want

I wish, I wish, I wish—
it's the sound of the blood's own steady breath,
the lungs' airy wax and wane,
the heart's secret metre.

Where is the shaman
to snip harmless cuttings
of seasonal luck,
coax rootlets of stubborn health
to stretch and grip
in the body's winter bed?

I wish, I wish, I wish
words on tongue, page, screen
would seed a wellness as bold
as our kowhai in spring
when it stands proud-bellied
as a woman in pregnancy
and in its leaves a thousand yellow flowers
glitter and sway
as if the sun were a flock of pilgrims
who have pinned trinkets, bells, sequins to her skirts

Our Lady of Blossoms
Our Lady of Fantails and Waxeyes
Our Lady of Summers Past, and Now, and Still to Come.

Brood

Just when our youngest has learned to say 'Duck!'
to the right picture in *This Little Chick*,
the city preens itself with his first spring.

On the inlet, four small ducklets trail drake and hen.
Daily miracles! Small wonders!
The baby is amazed. He points. 'Duck!'
There is a real thing for the sound we make.
'Duck!' As if the word spills a spell,
the world paddles off the page.

Like brilliant pupils on the snow slopes
the birdlings carve right inside their parents' glittering wakes,
loop on cue in a quiet queue,
so light and fluent in the language of float
they could be four downy balls threaded on one string,
or smoke from Donald's cigar, puffed in four perfect rings.

Look, look, and we all sing the one-word song again: 'Duck!'
Which is when the picture flings apart
with a frantic rush of duck and gull,
a dervish whirl, a scimitar dance of wing-bones, beak edge,
we'd even swear antlers, hooves, in a clash of stags
as the air grates and wrenches with their cries …

Then all of an undone flurry, calm comes down again,
though we can't see how:
mother duck and father duck
must have swallowed burning chaos
right along their feather-coated throats,
for the gull, snarling-ugly, just squats and waddles in troll-like circles
before it veers its sneering way away.

We count the plucky ducklings.
Four adored! Order restored!
A quartet of pom-poms leads our cheers
as the lesson resumes: kick and swim, scud and drift.

But the following day, a slice of night:
on our outing, we see only three duck-chicks,
and the next, just two—which is when the countdown ends,
for we've not wanted to walk that way again,
to teach subtraction before our youngest
even knows his numbers,
to witness the parents turn and turn in place,
the water spread around them too sheet-like, too smooth.

Snails

The potato patch, abandoned while we've been busy on other things,
has turned a little eccentric,
dressed itself in weeds like a widow's, though green,
and like the so-called lonely
definitely dippy old dear
I'm likely to be,
has thickened at the waist, loosened its stays,
taken in an entire colony of waifs and strays:
become a favourite of snails.

They seem to live at a standstill, though they teem:
so something must have moved
at least a few of them,
made them loony-blind enough with urges
to jump one another millimetre by millimetre
(being creepy surely a good thing in snails)
and it does seem they're only as impassive as stones
until they're collected,
when they're like knucklebones
that suddenly sprout aerials:
little brown radios spinning their dials for news
of what disaster has just picked up their houses,
made them foam at their one long foot
like rabid mixed-up mutts,
or squids that spit ink blots
as if to say their enemies really need a shrink
to help defuse their atavistic aggression issues …

Speaking of which,
because a million pressing things these days
mean I'm not very Zen
but also lack a hunter's pragmatism
and the moral fibre
of my grandfather's generation
who would say it was my duty
to finish off these umpteen soft-in-the-heads,
to stove in the substandard safety helmets

of this lazy plague of unicyclists
who could take a whole day
to push-pedal across the road—
because, that is, I'm a dozen kinds of coward
who should have written this poem first
to really think things through—
I neither salt nor poison them
nor pulp them with my red gumshoes
but pluck each snail off its leaf,
and with my best, yes, out-in-left-field baseball arm
launch each one in a fierce brilliant arc
towards the leaf-plump, song-filled trees,
calling out, 'Now you're free!'

Suddenly they're gymnasts, aerialists,
and as they leap a few evolutionary rungs
I'm sure I can hear the small voices inside
those home-grown, one-pilot cock-pits: 'I can fly!'

I like to think
that's how they've always dreamed of going:
out on a high note,
and that's it, isn't it?
That's the delusion
that gets many of us through:

that there will be a giant hand
that cradles us for a moment,
then transports us beyond ourselves,
beyond all science and reason,
beyond our maddest scribbles, screwiest dreams,
to where, in a champagne rush, we reach a euphoric revelation
that fries our tiny minds before we even feel the fall …

But for now? For now, the weeds are gone,
the soil's freshly turned,
and they could be speaking Greek,
for all I know, Virginia,
but the birds sound happy:
happy as a box of themselves, released:
happy as Mohammeds whose mountains,
whose molehills, whose tiny, snail-sized desires
have—illogical, zoological miracles—come to them.

Well

Afterwards, I stood with my child
on the river's bridge
over the storm-swollen rapids.

Make your two wishes, he said,
and into my hands he pressed
shredded petals he'd found, fallen
from the peach-silk hot house flowers
he calls 'the singing plant'
for their glorious, open mouths.

Their colour flared like tossed coins
towards the river's turbulent surface:
on contact still they burnt a moment
like soft metal lit by air—
then were pulled beneath the bridge and gone.

What did you wish? he asked, as we walked on—
and I could have confessed each one:
your name, and what I wanted, still want
to have you choose to say: but then as good admit

I wished to be like water:
able to take whatever fractures it—
floodwrack, oar-thrust, fish leap,
the birds' swift javelin stabs
as they hurtle down and pierce its skin—
and to then as smoothly mend again,
unmarred,
as if the mind could be its own physician.

Rootstock

There is a street in our suburb
that garners prizes: a small plaque tells us
in the past it's won Best Kept,
with its lawns laid out like picnic rugs,
its lush trees, tight-trimmed hedges,
its figurines of Chinamen with fishing rods,
donkeys with panniers, its trellis arcs and wagon wheels:
mass-produced tat, it seems to me,
though clearly some committee
thought it hit the apex of streetliness,
and that like the A&P show's roundest sow,
plumpest pumpkin, lambiest lamb, or most gorgeous courgette,
this is it: this is what we, the human race can achieve,
if we'd all put our trowels, shears, mowers, hammers, secateurs, trailers, gift
                                                                                                       vouchers
and our hearts, our hearts to the streets!

And although there is one garden that brims over its borders,
fans out its lilies, delphiniums, petunias and roses
like the urgent, shaking tail of a bachelor peacock,
its gardener a dirt-artist, an earth-sorcerer,
who can stun me in my tracks as I crest the hill to see his works,

my favourite place faces opposite,
where among huddles of thorny weeds, and shrubs that sprout brown
                                                                                                         sticks,
someone's dumped odd, blackened, box-like hulls of paint-chipped metal,
an empty, blue suitcase yanked open like a scoured-out clam,
and a dozen bulging rubbish bags
that loll against each other like overfed pups
or obese museum guards bored-drunk on duty.

And although its neighbours do grow flowers
as shimmering and pert and quick and smart
as Head Girls or Double Duxes, it's not tall poppy envy,
this attraction to the rumpled, unkempt, unshaven,
devil-come-here-and-let-me-lick-the-butter-from-your-chin look,

but gratitude for the blunt statement
that sometimes things get broken, or burnt, are ugly, don't work,
they hurt, the head and heart overwhelmed, a tangled, rat-king paradox
of sorrow, anger, loss, and who gives a toss, who cares, who cares who sees?

The Truth Garden, let's call it,
and every piece of trash slumped there
the tough rootstock of honesty.

Proposal

With his hands on her hips
as if in an ice dance
he suggests in the tone
of a man who has just said
let's move the blue armchair
closer to the window
so we can bring the hills
into the frame

let's have another baby

and it's like that moment
in the drink-sped conversation
at a bar in a town far from home
when the too-handsome stranger
drew out an edge of silver
like a ring to catch the light
then asking her how she liked her sex
pressed the knife's metal tongue
to the flicker at her throat
as gently as if a child were dressing her neck
with threaded stalks, white petals

and it's the moment walking past
an unlit downtown doorway
when footsteps start their time-bomb tick
behind you:

stay calm, she thinks,
no sudden moves

Charm

She sees a button, picks it up
throughout the day, thinks bad luck.

Small round token of the undone,
it brings to mind
desire fumbled or unrequited,
conversations interrupted,
manuscripts unfinished.

She imagines the almond-eyed gap
that misses its fill,
thinks of someone never quite warm enough,
or unevenly dressed,
like a child not fully tucked in at night
who chases sleep from side to side,
nearly catches it but then it lifts
like a tissue-paper crown on the wind.

Solo tiddlywink with no one to leapfrog,
little kite that's lost its string,
it sits like a cuckoo's egg in her wallet's nest
the size of a coin that can't be spent,
yet so smooth and tight in its shiny skin
it insists it must be the seed of something:
say, a wild, honey-scented shrub
that rumplestiltskins soil and sun
into soft, cotton heads
that bloom and gleam like daytime moons
at the window of a seaside crib.

Months later, the button still sits with her change:
as if one day the garment it fled
might spindrift into her garden,
silky storm-bird blown off course—

though it seems the button's burning colour
is what's really earned its keep:

watch how she holds it up to the light and smiles

as if happiness has been boiled down to a bead,
a vitamin for the heart by way of the eye:

minuscule, rose-tinted monocle,
compact, pocket-sized fortune's wheel—
see how that bad luck's turned?

Little Drummer Boy

He's picking up percussion so quickly
he could almost be bilingual in drums:
while we've gentled the young buck of him in English
rhythm's given him another native tongue.

By ear, by sun-spill, by moonrise,
by wind-light, by leaf-shift, by fireside,
he's caught the daily cadence
of feet up and down the hours,
the pom-tee-pom-tiddly-pom
of opening windows and doors,
and the sudden, rilling fill
from the clear solo of rainfall.

Whenever there's a small, still patch of silence
in his full-tilt days,
his fingertips dart with fidgets—
he fiddlesticks beats on chair-backs, his knees,
kicks and knocks invisible floor toms
as if they're gas pedals to give time speed.

In any margin of quiet he finds
his hands just have to doodle
the aural loops and twirls
of everything he's thinking—
a boom-badda-boom of comets, trees, stars,
a snash-snash, be-dup-swang-swang
of Lego, space travel, vampire fangs.

The deep-down thrumming hum of him
auditions every surface as his drum-skin;
he taps so much he's split his nails,
his fingertips feel raw—
but the be-doom-doom-be dap in him
insists he tips this *I'm alive!* high-hat
to anything passing by:
sparrows, strangers, day-sky, grey-sky,
rubbish truck, brother, fog-cat, snow-sky …

hey, paradiddle dumpling,
here's our son's song:

buddy hit the kettle drums,
buddy hit the table drums,
buddy hit the cupboard drums,
the world is there to play.

Mind's Eye

For Rhys Brookbanks

The left lid tics, jittered feather,
like a body's small aftershocks
as sobs subside into sleep.

This tic won't tack, won't stop,
it seems to track *untruth*:
blink and smiles lie,
calm storms, blanks are drawn;
speak bright and brave
but the eye's flicker signals no,
fear and fazed,
takes each simple fact and twitches it
like a magician's trick silks
collapsed to cold air.

General wisdom dismisses it as tiredness,
mind pitched at overwork, overdrive,
but the eye wants to shut out what it can't see,
the mind wants this blank to be REM sleep.

Lashes judder, heart's arrhythmia,
the lens of a camera that stammers with dark
because *now* is caught so hard on *then*.

The lid trembles like a lip,
like a drop brink-tipped,
like the papers in our hands
as we're forced to read your name.

Friend, the body mourns
in its own Morse.
The sight shakes.

Seismograph

When I was sure the virus-stunned, weepy child
was tucked properly under his covers,
and I scrubbed the sick from his car seat and our rugs
with hot, soapy water from the big green bucket
and carried away the solid pail as carefully
as I would the sleeping infant himself,

I was thinking mothers, Nightingales, fevers, night shifts;
fathers, forms haunch-hunkered, hands on scorching foreheads;
the shape of tenderness, a parent's spine fern-stooped in a darkened room;
the way the self's time must slow to the sore clock of a child's body.

So when the big green bucket dropped
from its crappy plastic handle, smashed,
and flung a flood of sick-soaked water
over my hair, face, clothes,
the walls, window, floor and doors,

I took a deep breath and thought,
it's nothing, we're all safe, it's small stuff,
they always say, don't sweat the small stuff,
but then, with the inaudible tug
of some last filament splintering
the clear and obvious thought fell open

that as you grew, someone scrubbed and cleaned,
ferried and carried, bent and lifted for you:
and there, right there, the hurt bird of rage flew;
I was off my own handle, I sweated it, all of it, I spat piss and fucks,
I took that crapped-out, senseless bucket
and broke it open again with both fists,
I re-broke it over my knees, rammed it with a heel,
snapped it like rotten, useless sticks,
shoved it in the bin and bawled
that it was a stupid piece of shit, gone, finished—

but then, with my adult tantrum spent,
still I was left with the space between curses
and the curses burnt on my mouth,
the shiver at the dusk-skinned window,
the invisible pressure the edges of everything—
metal taps, laundry sink, child's face in retinal image—
only just keep at bay:
the thing we cannot break
in our bare, wet, shaken hands.
For your death still sat and stared back,
everywhere, like the air.

Mourning Song

I know a man who greets the news of each familiar death
with a gladdened, emphatic, 'Good!'
as if someone close, after long prevarication,
has reached the right decision,
or been accepted for some prestigious course,
or for a job they've fought and longed for,
and which everyone who loves them knows
they will shine at, having come into their own
like a newborn lifted to the spotlight of the first smile it's shown,
or an understudy gifted the diva's role.

And although I can't believe him,
nor share his fresh-scrubbed optimism
at his work in ritual bewitchments,
such as the way he passes pretty, polished, moon-shaped stones
over the hurt or heart-lost to cure them,

as I grow older and watch both my children
push through the wax and wane of phase on phase,
when this man refuses to mourn
and I find my fears dig in their heels
while some tiny, tousled goblin in me gulps for air
to feed a foulsome, grief-riven howl,

more and more I wonder if
there isn't something in this of the small child
dragged through the thick thorns of its own ill will,
who kicks and bucks and bites to a bath
she knows she doesn't need, and which already fills
her very cells with *sick* and *hate* and *loathe*,
and yet who, within seconds in the clarifying water
grows calm, afloat, splash-happy,
delicious oblivion in little drips all over her skin.

Late

The sun in a medallion on the harbour
its rhythmic flicker caught like a lyric
from the radio of a passing car …

all the fragments of you I know
stacked up against those I never will—

what your thoughts are, along the shore,
hands in pockets, the dog ferreting the wind's scent
in the shadows of those stony cliffs:

your memory's loop back to which garden,
what rooms, the words and gazes held there

and how, say, the pear tree seemed
to frame and gloss the promises, sift them

for falsity, for charm; how perhaps
the burr of traffic, pippit of bird calls

sang like evidence of the future still being spun
from its own fingers, time distilled

yet moving, still moving, where would it carry you,
sweet young boy that you must have been,

how now will I ever know you
given I wasn't there,

in the imagined light, under the story's birdsong,
the fabular pear's lattice of temporary shadows

tracing lost time along your collarbone?

Heron Blue

Throughout these days of stoop, lift,
wear care like a scar-burnt skin,
and hope inside hope along hope
that all you do and fail to do
together somehow still make a frame
to hold the children safe enough that they may climb
up past the broken, flaw-riddled trellis of you
to sprout green, love-leavened selves
that can freight their own happiness
as weightless and brave as blossom—

all throughout, the island's birds
signal like flecks of sun on glass.
Swans, heads bowed, seem to cradle
thought to themselves.
Slender shags slice the silver water once,
then are gone.
Terns spring like eros-white darts
across a heron-blue sky,
while the herons shake like flames
even in the wake of your own slow walk.

Their images ripple quietly across deep memory
like the name of a love so covert
it is hardly recognised as desire;
a name that lifts on the lip of sleep,
or as you drive along the blinding gold harbour,
or the hill city's lights press at the dusk
like a choir of candles in a cathedral dark.

These birds, they remind you
of the one still hidden
who couldn't tell anyone,
not even the beloved,
that you loved, and how.
Spindle-shaped, fleet and narrow
they flit from sky to sky, night to night,
bright shuttles that mend and mend again
each day's torn seams.

Instructions for a Karitane Solo:
How to Use this Crib

For Noel Waite and Amanda Floyd

Like a coffee cup left out on the lawn,
gather raindrops, catch birdsong.

Feel the sun slip down from the sky's white shell,
let ants and green-backed, shimmer-skinned beetles

track up over your shoulders' rim,
let petals and leaves brush past as they fall.

Wait, patient as the small jade figurine of a Buddha
lost in long grass on another island years ago:

as light trickles over you

hold yourself in the palm
of your own thoughts

bead of water
in the throat of a rose.

ACKNOWLEDGEMENTS

Acknowledgements are due to the editors, judges, or event organisers who have selected individual poems here for: *Best New Zealand Poems 2009*; *Deep South*; *Dublin Review*; *Harvard Review*; *International Literary Quarterly*; *Landfall*; *Listener*; *New Zealand Books*; *Otago Daily Times*; *Poems in the Waiting Room Competition 2012* ('An Inward Sun', first place); *Poetry Daily* website; *Red Wheelbarrow*; *Some Shells in a Tobacco Tin: Ruth Dallas Tribute*, New Zealand Electronic Poetry Centre; *New Zealand Society of Authors Chapbook*; *New Zealand Studies Association Bulletin of New Zealand Studies*; *Takahe*; *Takahe* Poetry Competition 2008 ('Well', first place); *Trout*; *Trust*: Caselberg Trust Poetry and Jewellery Collaboration (with John Z Robinson—'Event!'). 'Girls' High' and 'Good Morning, Miss' are responses to a visual arts proposal from designer Amy Thorburn.